START
Listening

The Wobbly Wand

Clare Bevan

QED Publishing

Copyright © QED Publishing 2005

First published in the UK in 2005 by
QED Publishing
A Quarto Group company
226 City Road
London EC1V 2TT
www.qed-publishing.co.uk

A Catalogue record for this book is available from the British Library.

ISBN 1 84538 145 9

Written by Clare Bevan
Designed by Melissa Alaverdy
Editor Hannah Ray
Illustrated by Gary De La Cour

Series Consultant Anne Faundez
Publisher Steve Evans
Creative Director Louise Morley
Editorial Manager Jean Coppendale

Printed and bound in China

**Books should be returned on or before the
last date stamped below.**

Cast List

Teddy Bear (narrator)

Toy Mouse

Toy Duck

Toy Frog

Toy Dog

Fairy Doll

Setting

The play takes place in a playroom. To start, all the toys are fast asleep. Fairy Doll is peeping out of a toy box. She holds a wobbly wand. Half-hidden in the toy box is a shiny, new wand. Teddy Bear, wearing glasses, is sitting on a chair, reading this book.

Props

- A wobbly wand
- A straight wand
- A chair
- A pair of glasses
- A cardboard box (for the toy box)

Teddy Bear: The girls and boys have gone to bed,
So now the toys can play instead.

Mouse: (*Jumping up*) Squeak! Squeak!

Duck: (*Jumping up*) Quack! Quack!

Frog: (*Jumping up*) Croak! Croak!

Dog: (*Jumping up*) Bark! Bark!

Mouse: Hooray! The playroom's warm and dark.

Duck: It's time to flap … (*flaps arms*)

Frog: And hop about … (*hops up and down*)

Dog: And run, run, run … (*runs about*)

Fairy Doll: (*Popping up from the toy box*)
But PLEASE don't shout.
Don't rush around and make a noise.
We MUSTN'T wake the girls and boys.

Teddy Bear: The toys are having LOTS of fun.

Mouse: (*Waving at window*) Hello moon, and goodbye sun.

Duck: Chase me!

Frog: Catch me!

Dog: Run, run, run!

(*The toys play noisily.*)

Fairy Doll: I'll have to stop them with a spell.
I hope my wand is working well.

(*Fairy Doll waves her wobbly wand.*)

Teddy Bear: Her wobbly wand goes flip, flap, flop.

Fairy Doll: Toys! BE QUIET! Silence! Stop!

(*The toys stand very still.*)

Fairy Doll: I'll make your voices soft as rain. Wake up, toys, and speak again.

(*The toys start to wriggle.*)

Teddy Bear: The midnight sky is darkest blue, But ALL the toys can say is …

All the toys: MOO!

(*The toys all look puzzled.*)

Duck: Moo, moo?

Mouse: Moo, moo?

Frog: Moo, moo?

Dog: Moooo?

Mouse: Where's my squeak?

| Duck: | And where's my quack? |
| Frog and Dog: | Fairy! Bring our voices back! |

Fairy Doll: I'll try to make the magic stop …

(She wobbles her wand. The toys stand still.)

But still my wand goes flip, flap, FLOP!

(The toys start to wriggle.)

Teddy Bear: The moon is shining bright as day, But ALL the toys can say is …

All the toys: Neigh!

(They gallop about like horses.)

Neigh, neigh. Neigh, neigh. Neigh, neigh. NEIGH!

Mouse:	Where's my squeak?
Duck:	And where's my quack?
Frog and Dog:	Fairy! Bring our voices back!

Fairy Doll: I'll try to make the magic stop ...

(*She wobbles her wand. The toys stand still.*)

But STILL my wand goes flip, flap, FLOP!

(*The toys start to wriggle.*)

BAA!

Teddy Bear:	High above, there shines a star, But ALL the toys can say is …
All the toys:	BAA! *(They crawl around on all fours like sheep.)* Baa, baa. Baa, baa. Baa, baa. BAAAAA! *(The Fairy Doll looks very sorry.)*
Mouse:	Where's my squeak?
Duck:	And where's my quack?
Frog and Dog:	Fairy! Bring our voices back!

13

Fairy Doll: I'll try to make the magic stop.

(*She wobbles her wand. The toys stand still.*)

But STILL my wand goes flip, flap, FLOP.

(*The toys start to wriggle.*)

Teddy Bear: The sky is darker than before,
But ALL the toys can say is ...

All the toys: ROAR!

(*They prowl around like lions.*)

Roar, roar. Roar, roar, Roar, roar. ROAR!

(*The Fairy Doll looks very upset.*)

Mouse:	Where's my squeak?
Duck:	And where's my quack?
Frog and Dog:	Fairy! Bring our voices back!

Fairy Doll: My spells won't work.
What CAN I do?
I WISH my wand could be
BRAND NEW.

(*She jumps into the toy box.*)

Teddy Bear: She throws her wobbly wand away,
And fairy music starts to play.

(*Tinkly music plays.*)

Mouse: A magic time!

Duck: A magic sound!

Frog: We hop and jump!

Dog: And spin around.

(*Fairy Doll pops up with the new wand.*)

Fairy Doll: My wand's brand new! Hip hooray!

Teddy Bear: I wonder what the toys will say?

All the toys:	Croak! Bark! Squeak! Quack!
Mouse:	I've found my squeak!
Duck:	I've found my quack!
Frog and Dog:	At last! We've got our voices back!
Mouse:	We'll only make a LITTLE noise.
Duck:	We won't wake up the girls and boys.

Fairy Doll:	We'll play a very QUIET game.
Teddy Bear:	They tiptoed round till morning came, And when they saw the golden sun, They said …
All the toys:	Goodbye! To EVERYONE!

(They wave and bow – and fall asleep.)

Can you squeak like a mouse?
Can you croak like a frog?

Do frogs usually say 'baa'? What sort of animal says 'baa'?

The wobbly wand
wasn't very good at
spells. What did it do?

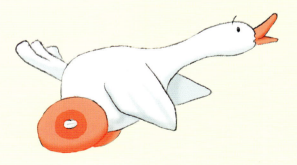

Can you find a
word that rhymes
with 'quack'?

21

Sometimes the toys are quiet.
Can you be a quiet dog?

Why didn't Fairy Doll
want the other toys to
make a noise?

Can you be a VERY
noisy duck?

Do frogs usually say 'moo'?
What kind of animal makes
a 'moo' sound?

Parents' and teachers' notes

- Play a rhyming game with your child. Can your child find a rhyme for 'frog'? Or 'toy'?

- Read lines from the script, practising different voices. Can your child talk in a doggy voice? Have fun trying out different voices for each of the different characters.

- Read the script and practise reading with expression. Can your child make his or her voice sound cross? (Like Fairy Doll at the start of the play.) Can your child sound happy? (Like the toys at the end of the play.)

- Look at the lines in the playscript that are in italics. Explain to your child that these lines are stage directions and that they tell the actors what to do while they are saying their lines. Explain that the stage directions are not read aloud.

- Practise reading lines from the play, emphasizing the words in capital letters. What effect does this have? Does it make the play more dramatic?

- Experiment with making different facial expressions to match different lines in the play. Can your child pull a cross face? Can your child look puzzled, like the toys when they all say 'moo'?

- Hunt around your house or school for real instruments (drums, whistles, shakers and glockenspiels) or make your own instruments (for example, from keys, tins and saucepans). Invent sound effects for the wobbly wand, and some tinkly music for when the toys hear the magic sound. When your child is pleased with the music, record it and then play it back. Does it work? Could it be even more magical?

- Can your child think of any occasions when he or she has to be quiet, for example, in a library, when a baby brother or sister is asleep or when playing hide and seek?

- Make a list of sounds your child likes. Why does he or she like them?

- Choose a piece of music for the end of the play and enjoy it together.

- Have fun putting the play together as a performance. Play the part of Teddy Bear (the narrator) yourself and emphasize the end-rhymes. This will help the 'actors' to guess what is coming next (for example, 'back' – 'quack', 'blue' – 'moo', 'day' – 'neigh').